Hexavalent Chromium

U.S. Department of Labor

Occupational Safety and Health Administration

OSHA 3373-10
2009

Contents

Introduction . . . 3

Worker Exposure and Health Consequences . . . 5

OSHA's Hexavalent Chromium Standards . . . 5

Exposure Limits . . . 6

Exposure Monitoring and Determinations . . . 6

Scheduled Monitoring Option . . . 7

Regulated Areas . . . 10

Control Measures . . . 10

Requirements for Protective Work
Clothing and Equipment . . . 12

Hygiene Areas and Practices . . . 14

Housekeeping . . . 15

Medical Surveillance . . . 16

Worker Training and Communication . . . 19

Recordkeeping . . . 20

Effective Dates . . . 22

Additional Information . . . 22

References . . . 23

OSHA Assistance . . . 24

OSHA Regional Offices . . . 28

Introduction

This document is intended to supplement OSHA's Small Entity Compliance Guide for the Hexavalent Chromium Standards published in 2006 (see Additional Information section for web link to this document) and to give readers an overview of the provisions and requirements of the Hexavalent Chromium standards for general industry (29 CFR 1910.1026), shipyards (29 CFR 1915.1026), and construction (29 CFR 1926.1126).

Hexavalent chromium (Cr(VI)) is a toxic form of the element chromium. Hexavalent chromium is rarely found in nature and is generally man-made. Cr(VI) is widely used in pigments, metal finishing (electroplating), wood preservatives and fungicides, and in chemical synthesis as an ingredient and catalyst. Table 1 on the next page lists some selected Cr(VI) compounds with their synonyms and common uses.

Hexavalent chromium may also be present in fumes generated during the production or welding of chrome alloys. Chromium metal is often alloyed with other metals or plated on metal and plastic substrates to improve corrosion resistance and provide protective coatings. The steel Industry is a major consumer of chromium metal in the production of stainless steel.

This booklet is intended to provide information about the Hexavalent Chromium standards for general industry (29 CFR 1910.1026), shipyards (29 CFR 1915.1026), and construction (29 CFR 1926.1126). The *Occupational Safety and Health Act* requires employers to comply with safety and health standards promulgated by OSHA or by a state with an OSHA-approved state plan. However, this booklet is not itself a standard or regulation, and it creates no new legal obligations.

Since 2000, there has been a decline in the use of chromates in pigments for paints and coatings; printing inks; ceramic, glass and construction materials; roofing and plastics. Employers are substituting less toxic inorganic and organic pigments where possible (SRI Consulting, 2008).

Table 1. Selected Cr(VI) Compounds and Their Uses

Chemical Name	*Synonyms*	*Uses*
Chromium Trioxide	Chromic acid, chromia, chromic (VI) acid, chromic trioxide, chromium oxide, chromium (VI) oxide	Most common uses: chromium plating, aluminum anodizing, and chemical intermediate for chromated copper arsenate wood preservatives. Other uses: ceramic glazes, colored glass, metal cleaning, inks, and paints (inorganic pigments).
Lead Chromate	C.I. pigment Yellow 34, crocoite, lead chromium oxide, plumbous chromate	Decorating china, pigment in industrial paints, rubber and plastics, pigment in oil paints and watercolors, and printing fabrics.
Sodium Dichromate	Disodium salt, chromium sodium oxide, dichromic acid, disodium dichromate, sodium bichromate, sodium dichromate	Inks, oxidizing agent in the manufacture of dyes and many other synthetic organic chemicals, electric batteries, manufacture of chromic acid, other chromates and chrome pigments, corrosion inhibiting paints, component of wood preservatives, and colorant for glass.
Zinc Chromate	Zinc salt, chromium zinc oxide, zinc chromium oxide, zinc tetraoxychromate	Priming paints for metals, varnishes and pigments in aerospace paints.

Adapted from: Meridian Research, 1994.

Worker Exposure and Health Consequences

Workplace exposure to Cr(VI) may cause the following health effects:

- lung cancer in workers who breathe airborne Cr(VI);
- irritation or damage to the nose, throat and lungs (respiratory tract) if Cr(VI) is inhaled; and
- irritation or damage to the eyes and skin if Cr(VI) contacts these organs.

Workers can inhale airborne Cr(VI) as a dust, fume or mist while, among other things, producing chromate pigments, dyes and powders (such as chromic acid and chromium catalysts); working near chrome electroplating; performing hot work and welding on stainless steel, high chrome alloys and chrome-coated metal; and applying and removing chromate-containing paints and other surface coatings. Skin exposure can occur while handling solutions, coatings and cements containing Cr(VI).

OSHA'S Hexavalent Chromium Standards

OSHA has separate standards for Cr(VI) exposures in general industry, shipyards and construction. Most of the requirements are the same for all sectors, with the exception of provisions for regulated areas, hygiene areas and practices, and housekeeping. Where there are differences, they will be explained in this booklet. The standards generally apply to occupational exposures to Cr(VI) in all forms and compounds in general industry, shipyards and construction, with specific exceptions outlined in the box below. States that administer their own OSHA-approved occupational safety and health plans may have different requirements. See the Additional Information section for a list of State plans and their contact information.

The Cr(VI) standards do not apply in three situations:

- exposures that occur in the application of pesticides;
- exposures to Portland cement; and
- where the employer has objective data demonstrating that a material containing Cr(VI) or a specific process, operation, or activity involving Cr(VI) cannot release dusts, fumes or mists of Cr(VI) in concentrations at or above 0.5 micrograms per cubic meter ($\mu g/m^3$) of air as an 8-hour time-weighted average (TWA) under any expected conditions of use.

Exposure Limits

The final Cr(VI) rule establishes an 8-hour TWA permissible exposure limit (PEL) of 5 $\mu g/m^3$ measured as Cr(VI). This means that over the course of any 8-hour work shift, the average exposure to Cr(VI) cannot exceed 5 $\mu g/m^3$.

The Action Level is set at 2.5 $\mu g/m^3$ of Cr(VI) calculated as an 8-hour TWA.

Exposures above the Action Level trigger specific requirements, and exposures above the PEL trigger additional requirements. The substantive provisions of the Cr(VI) standard are described below.

Exposure Monitoring and Determinations

Each employer who has a workplace or work operation covered by the Cr(VI) standards must determine the 8-hour TWA exposure for each worker exposed to Cr(VI). To comply with this provision, employers can choose between two options for performing exposure determinations:

- a scheduled monitoring option; or
- a performance-oriented option.

When monitoring for Cr(VI), employers must use a method of monitoring and analysis that provides values within plus or minus

25 percent of the true value at least 95 percent of the time for airborne concentrations at or above the Action Level. Examples of methods that meet these criteria are OSHA method ID215 (version 2) and NIOSH methods 7600, 7604, 7605 and 7703.

Scheduled Monitoring Option

The Initial Monitoring

Employers who select the scheduled monitoring option must conduct initial exposure monitoring to determine exposure to Cr(VI) for each worker. This involves taking a sufficient number of personal breathing zone air samples to accurately characterize full shift exposure on each shift, for each job classification, in each work area. Monitoring results must indicate the worker's time-weighted average exposure to airborne Cr(VI) over a typical 8-hour workday.

In some cases the employer will need to monitor all exposed workers, while in other cases it will be sufficient to monitor "representative" personnel. Representative exposure sampling is permitted when a number of workers perform essentially the same job under the same conditions. For example, an employer may choose one welder to sample as a representative of several welders who work in a welding shop for determining exposure as long as all of the welders represented by the monitoring perform the same job under the same conditions. Representative personal sampling for workers engaged in similar work involving similar Cr(VI) exposures is achieved by monitoring the worker(s) reasonably expected to have the highest Cr(VI) exposures. For example, this may involve monitoring the Cr(VI) exposure of the worker closest to an exposure source. This exposure result may then be used to represent the exposure of other workers in the group. The employer must take at least one sample characteristic of the entire work shift or consecutive representative samples taken over the length of the shift.

Periodic Monitoring

Periodic monitoring is required if the initial monitoring shows that the worker's exposure is at or above the Action Level (See

Table 2, below, for monitoring frequency.)

Table 2. Monitoring Frequency

Exposure Scenario	Required Monitoring Activity
Below the Action Level (< 2.5 μg/m³)	No periodic monitoring required for workers represented by the initial monitoring.
At or above the Action Level but at or below the PEL (2.5 μg/m³ to 5 μg/m³)	Monitor every six months.
Above the PEL (> 5 μg/m³)	Monitor every three months.

If initial monitoring shows exposures above the PEL, but subsequent periodic measurements indicate that exposures have fallen to levels at or below the PEL, but still above the Action Level, the employer may reduce the frequency of periodic monitoring to every six months. In addition, an employer may discontinue periodic monitoring for workers represented by monitoring results indicating that exposures have fallen below the Action Level if those results are confirmed by a second measurement taken at least seven days later.

Additional Monitoring

Additional monitoring is necessary when a workplace change may result in new or additional exposures to Cr(VI) or the employer has any reason to believe that new or additional exposures have occurred. These changes may include alterations in the production process, raw materials, equipment, personnel, work practices, or control methods used in the workplace.

Examples of Situations Requiring Additional Monitoring
Example 1: If an employer has conducted monitoring for an electroplating operation while using fume suppressants, and the use of fume suppressants is discontinued, then additional monitoring

would be necessary to determine worker exposures under the modified conditions.

Example 2: A welder may move from an open, outdoor location to an enclosed or confined space. Even though the task performed and materials used may remain constant, the changed environment could reasonably be expected to result in higher exposures to Cr(VI).

Performance-Oriented Option

The performance-oriented option allows the employer to determine the 8-hour TWA exposure for each worker on the basis of any combination of air monitoring data, historical monitoring data, or objective data sufficient to accurately determine current worker exposure to Cr(VI). This option is intended to allow employers flexibility in assessing the Cr(VI) exposures of their personnel. Where the employer elects to use this option, the exposure determination must be performed prior to the time that the work operation commences and must provide the same degree of assurance that worker exposures have been correctly characterized as is provided for under the scheduled monitoring option. Like under the scheduled monitoring option, the employer is expected to reevaluate worker exposures when there is any change in the production process, raw materials, equipment, personnel, work practices, or control methods that may result in new or additional exposures to Cr(VI). However, the employer using the performance-oriented option does not have to follow any particular fixed schedule for performing reevaluations.

Objective Data

The Objective data means information that demonstrates the expected worker exposure to Cr(VI) associated with a particular product or material or a specific process, operation, or activity. Information that can serve as objective data includes, but is not limited to, air monitoring data from an industry-wide survey; data collected by a trade association from its members; or calculations based on the composition or chemical and physical properties of a material. The data must reflect workplace conditions closely resembling the processes, types of material, control methods, work practices and environmental conditions in the employer's current operations.

Regulated Areas

The Cr(VI) standard for general industry includes requirements for regulated areas wherever a worker's exposure to airborne concentrations of Cr(VI) is or is reasonably expected to be above the PEL. However, OSHA has not included this requirement in the construction and shipyard standards due to the expected practical difficulties of establishing regulated areas for operations in these sectors.

Employers are required to distinguish the regulated area from the rest of the workplace in a manner that adequately establishes and alerts workers to the boundaries of the regulated area. The standard does not specify how employers are to indicate the regulated areas. Warning signs, gates, ropes, barricades, lines, textured flooring, or other methods may be appropriate. Whatever methods are chosen must effectively warn workers not to enter the area unless they are authorized. Authorized personnel are those persons required by their job duties to be present in the area and may include maintenance/repair personnel, managers and quality control engineers. Also, designated worker representatives may enter the regulated area to observe exposure monitoring. All persons who enter the regulated area must use proper protective equipment, including respirators when appropriate.

Control Measures

To protect workers from Cr(VI) hazards, whenever exposures exceed the PEL employers must use engineering and work practice controls to reduce and maintain Cr(VI) exposures to or below the PEL. These are the most effective controls. Whenever feasible engineering and work practice controls are not sufficient to reduce exposures to or below the PEL, the employer must use such controls to reduce exposures to the lowest levels achievable and supplement them by the use of respiratory protection.

Engineering controls include substitution (using a less toxic material or process that results in lower exposures), isolation (such as enclosing the source of exposure), and ventilation (such as using a local exhaust system that captures airborne Cr(VI) near its source).

Work practice controls involve adjustments in the way a task is performed. Workers must know the proper way to perform a task in order to minimize their exposure and to maximize the effectiveness of the control. For example, a welder should be properly trained to correctly position himself and the local exhaust ventilation to minimize exposure to the welding fume. In many cases, work practice controls complement engineering controls in providing worker protection.

Employers are not permitted to rotate workers to different jobs as a means of achieving compliance with the PEL.

Exceptions to the general requirement for primary use of feasible engineering and work practice controls to reduce worker exposures to within permissible limits:

- In the aerospace industry, when workers are painting aircraft or large aircraft parts (e.g., the interior or exterior of whole aircraft, aircraft wings or tail sections, or comparably sized aircraft parts), the employer must use feasible engineering and work practice controls to reduce worker Cr(VI) exposures to levels at or below 25 μg/m³. The employer must supplement its engineering and work practice controls with respiratory protection to achieve the PEL.
- If the employer can demonstrate that a particular process or task does not result in worker exposures to Cr(VI) exceeding the PEL for 30 or more days during any 12 consecutive months, the employer is allowed to use any combination of

controls, including respirators alone, to achieve the PEL. Historical data, objective data, or exposure monitoring data may be used for this purpose.

Respiratory Protection

Employers are required to provide workers with respirators when feasible engineering and work practice controls are unable to reduce worker exposure to Cr(VI) to levels at or below the PEL. Respirators are required during:

- Work operations such as maintenance and repair activities for which engineering and work practice controls are not feasible;
- Emergencies (i.e., any occurrence that results or is likely to result in an uncontrolled release of Cr(VI) that is not an incidental release that can be controlled by workers in the immediate area or by maintenance personnel);
- Where workers are exposed above the PEL for fewer than 30 days per year and the employer has opted not to implement engineering/work practice controls to achieve the PEL;
- Periods necessary to install or implement feasible engineering and work practice controls; or
- Operations where all feasible engineering and work practice controls have been implemented but are not sufficient to reduce exposures to or below the PEL.

Where respirator use is required, the employer must establish a respiratory protection program in accordance with OSHA's Respiratory Protection standard (29 CFR 1910.134). The respiratory protection program addresses procedures for properly selecting, using and maintaining respirators in the workplace. OSHA has prepared the document, a *Small Entity Compliance Guide for the Revised Respiratory Protection Standard* (see the Additional Information section at page 22).

Requirements for Protective Work Clothing and Equipment

Employers are required to provide and ensure the proper use of appropriate protective clothing and equipment whenever a hazard evaluation of the workplace has identified that skin or eye contact with Cr(VI) presents or is likely to present a hazard to workers. Where such a hazard is identified, the employer must select the clothing and equipment needed to protect workers from Cr(VI) hazards. Some examples of protective clothing and equipment that may be necessary include, but are not limited to, gloves, aprons, coveralls, foot coverings and goggles. Normal street clothing and uniforms or other accessories that do not protect workers from Cr(VI) hazards are not considered protective clothing or equipment under the standard. Employers must provide and maintain the clothing and equipment at no cost to the worker.

The following precautions must be taken to protect workers and others who handle protective clothing and equipment:

- The employer must ensure that workers remove protective clothing and equipment that has become contaminated with Cr(VI) either at the end of their work shift or when they complete their tasks involving Cr(VI) exposure, whichever comes first.

- The employer must not allow any worker to remove contaminated protective clothing or equipment from the workplace, except for those workers whose job it is to launder, clean, maintain, or dispose of the clothing or equipment.

- When contaminated protective clothing or equipment is removed for laundering, cleaning, maintenance or disposal, the employer must ensure that it is stored and transported in sealed, impermeable bags or other closed, impermeable containers.

- Bags or containers of contaminated protective clothing or equipment that are removed from change rooms for laundering, cleaning, maintenance or disposal must be labeled in accordance with OSHA's Hazard Communication standard at 29 CFR 1910.1200.

- The employer must clean, launder, repair and replace protective clothing and equipment as necessary to ensure that the effectiveness of the clothing and equipment is maintained.

- The employer must inform any person who launders or cleans protective clothing or equipment contaminated with Cr(VI) of the potentially harmful effects of Cr(VI) exposure, and that the clothing and equipment should be laundered or cleaned in a manner that minimizes skin or eye contact with Cr(VI) and prevents exposure to Cr(VI) in excess of the PEL. Removal of Cr(VI) from protective clothing and equipment by blowing, shaking, or any other means that disperses Cr(VI) into the air or onto a worker's body is prohibited.

Hygiene Areas and Practices

The Cr(VI) standards include requirements for change rooms, washing facilities, and eating and drinking areas to minimize exposure to Cr(VI). They are:

Change rooms are only required when workers must change out of their street clothes to use protective clothing and equipment. The change rooms must conform to 29 CFR 1910.141 (for general industry and shipyards) and 29 CFR 1926.51 (for construction), prevent Cr(VI) contamination of street clothes, and be equipped with separate storage facilities for protective clothing and equipment and for street clothes. This provision is intended to limit exposures after the work shift ends and avoid the contamination of workers' cars and homes.

Washing facilities must be provided and must be readily accessible and capable of removing Cr(VI) from the skin. Washing facilities must comply with OSHA's sanitation requirements at 29 CFR 1910.141 (for general industry), 29 CFR 1926.51 (for construction), and 29 CFR 1915.97 (for shipyards). The employer must ensure that affected workers use these facilities when necessary. This includes making sure that workers who have skin contact with Cr(VI) wash their hands and faces at the end of the work shift and prior to eating, drinking, smoking, chewing tobacco or gum, applying cosmetics, or using the toilet.

Eating and drinking areas and surfaces must conform with 29 CFR 1910.141 (for general industry), 29 CFR 1926.51 (for construction), and 29 CFR 1915.97 (for shipyards) and be maintained as free as practicable of Cr(VI) whenever employers allow workers to consume food or beverages at a worksite where Cr(VI) is present. Employers are also required to ensure that workers do not enter eating and drinking areas wearing protective clothing or equipment, unless the protective clothing or equipment is properly cleaned beforehand. Employers may use any method for removing surface Cr(VI) from clothing and equipment that does not disperse the dust into the air or onto the worker's body. For example, if a worker is wearing coveralls for protection against Cr(VI), thorough HEPA vacuuming of the coveralls could be performed prior to entry into a lunchroom. **Do NOT blow dust off protective clothing and equipment.**

The employer must ensure that workers do not eat, drink, smoke, chew tobacco or gum, or apply cosmetics – or carry or store products associated with these activities – in regulated areas or in areas where skin or eye contact with Cr(VI) occurs.

Housekeeping

The Cr(VI) standard for general industry includes housekeeping measures. OSHA did not include these requirements in the construction and shipyard standards due to the expected practical difficulties of complying with such requirements in those sectors. Proper housekeeping requirements are important because they target sources of exposure to Cr(VI) that engineering controls are generally not designed to address (such as skin exposures). Employers must ensure that all surfaces are maintained as free as practicable of accumulations of Cr(VI). Spills and releases of Cr(VI)-containing material must be cleaned up promptly. The requirement to maintain surfaces "as free as practicable" is performance-oriented. The standard does not specify what an allowable surface loading of Cr(VI) contamination in work areas would be. Instead, the requirement for "as free as practicable" is met when the employer is vigilant in efforts to ensure that surfaces are kept free of accumulation of Cr(VI) dust. OSHA will consider the employer's housekeeping schedule, the possibility of exposure from the surfaces in question, and the characteristics of the workplace. (OSHA, Jan. 13, 2003, Letter of Interpretation.)

Cleaning Methods

Surfaces contaminated with Cr(VI) must be cleaned by HEPA-filtered vacuuming or other methods that minimize exposure to

Cr(VI), including wet methods such as wet sweeping or wet scrubbing. Dry methods (e.g., dry shoveling, dry sweeping and dry brushing) are only allowed in cases where HEPA-filtered vacuuming or other methods that minimize the likelihood of exposure to Cr(VI) have been tried and found not to be effective. The use of compressed air for cleaning surfaces is only allowed when used in conjunction with a ventilation system designed to capture the dust cloud or when no alternative method is feasible. Employers should use caution whenever compressed air is used as a cleaning method, since the air will spread the contamination further unless the dust is appropriately collected. Compressed air should never be directed at workers and should not be used to clean protective clothing or equipment.

Employers must ensure that waste, scrap, debris and any other materials contaminated with Cr(VI) are collected and disposed of in sealed, impermeable bags or other closed, impermeable containers. Additionally, bags or containers of waste, scrap, debris and any other materials contaminated with Cr(VI) must be labeled in accordance with the requirements of the Hazard Communication standard, 29 CFR 1910.1200.

Medical Surveillance

The purpose of medical surveillance is to determine if an individual can be exposed to Cr(VI) at his or her workplace without experiencing adverse health effects; to identify Cr(VI)-related adverse health effects when they do occur so that appropriate intervention measures can be taken; and to determine a worker's fitness to use personal protective equipment such as respirators.

All medical examinations and procedures required by the standards must be performed by or under the supervision of a physician or other licensed healthcare professional (PLHCP). When medical surveillance is required it must be provided at no cost to workers and at a reasonable time and place. If participation requires travel away from the worksite, the employer must bear the cost. Workers must be paid for time spent taking medical examinations, including travel time.

Employers must provide medical surveillance to workers who are:

- Exposed or may be exposed to Cr(VI) at concentrations at or above the Action Level (as an 8-hour TWA) for 30 or more days per year;
- Experiencing signs and symptoms of adverse health effects associated with Cr(VI) exposures (e.g., blistering lesions, redness or itchiness of exposed skin, shortness of breath or wheezing that worsens at work, nosebleeds, a whistling sound while inhaling or exhaling); or
- Exposed in an emergency situation (i.e., any occurrence that results or is likely to result in an uncontrolled release of Cr(VI) that is not an incidental release that can be controlled by workers in the immediate area or by maintenance personnel).

Frequency of Medical Examination

Medical examinations must be given:

- Within 30 days after initial assignment to a job involving Cr(VI) exposure, unless the worker has received an examination that meets the requirements of the standard within the last 12 months;
- Annually;
- Within 30 days after a PLHCP's written medical opinion recommends an additional examination;
- Whenever a worker shows signs or symptoms of the adverse health effects associated with Cr(VI) exposure;
- Within 30 days after exposure during an emergency which results in an uncontrolled release of Cr(VI); or
- At the termination of employment, unless the last examination provided was less than six months prior to the date of termination.

Contents of the Medical Exams

- A medical and work history which focuses on: the worker's past, present and anticipated future exposure to Cr(VI); any history of respiratory system dysfunction; any history of asthma, dermatitis, skin ulceration or nasal septum perforation; and smoking status and history.
- A physical examination of the skin and respiratory tract.
- Any additional tests that the examining PLHCP considers appropriate for that worker.

Note: The standards do not specify tests or procedures that must be provided to all workers. Rather, the information obtained from the medical and work history along with the physical examination of the skin and respiratory tract (the main targets of Cr(VI) toxicity) allow the PLHCPs to use their medical judgment to determine what tests, if any, are warranted.

Information Provided to the PLHCP

The employer must ensure that the PLHCP has a copy of the Cr(VI) standard, and must provide the PLHCP with:

- A description of the affected worker's former, current and anticipated duties as they relate to Cr(VI) exposure;
- Information on the worker's former, current and anticipated Cr(VI) exposure levels;
- A description of any personal protective equipment used or to be used by the worker, including when and for how long the worker has used that equipment; and
- Information from records of employment-related medical examinations previously provided to the affected worker, currently within the control of the employer.

The Written Medical Opinion

The employer must obtain a written medical opinion from the PLHCP for each medical examination performed. The written medical opinion must be obtained within 30 days of the examination, and must contain:

- The PLHCP's opinion as to whether the worker has any detected medical condition(s) that would place the worker at increased risk of material impairment to health from further exposure to Cr(VI);
- Any recommended limitations on the worker's exposure to Cr(VI) or on the use of personal protective equipment such as respirators; and
- A statement that the PLHCP has explained to the worker the results of the medical examination, including any medical conditions related to Cr(VI) exposure that require further evaluation or treatment, and any special provisions for the use of protective clothing or equipment.

The PLHCP must not reveal to the employer any specific findings or diagnoses that are not related to workplace Cr(VI) exposure. The employer is required to provide a copy of the written medical opinion to the examined worker within two weeks after receiving it.

Worker Training and Communication

It is critically important that workers recognize the hazards associated with exposure to Cr(VI) and understand the measures they can take to protect themselves. OSHA's Hazard Communication standard (29 CFR 1910.1200) establishes requirements for employers to provide workers with information on hazardous chemicals such as Cr(VI) through comprehensive chemical hazard communication programs that include material safety data sheets (MSDSs), labels and worker training. Employers must follow the requirements of the Hazard Communication standard with regard to workers exposed to Cr(VI). These requirements include, but are not limited to, informing workers of any operations in their work area where Cr(VI) is present and training workers on the hazards of Cr(VI) and measures theys can take to protect themselves from these hazards (e.g., appropriate work practices, emergency procedures and protective equipment to be used).

In addition, the Cr(VI) standards require the employer to provide information and training sufficient to ensure that workers can demonstrate knowledge of:

- The requirements of the Cr(VI) standard; and
- The medical surveillance program required by the standard, including recognition of the signs and symptoms of adverse health effects that may result from Cr(VI) exposure.

The employer must also make a copy of the Cr(VI) standard available without cost to affected workers.

Recordkeeping

Accurate records can demonstrate employer compliance with the standard and can assist in diagnosing and identifying workplace-related illnesses. Therefore, employers are required to maintain records of worker Cr(VI) exposures (including air monitoring data, historical monitoring data and objective data) and medical surveillance records.

Air Monitoring Data

Employers must keep an accurate record of all air monitoring performed to comply with the standard. The record must indicate:

- The date of the measurement for each sample taken;
- The operation involving exposure to Cr(VI) that was monitored;
- Sampling and analytical methods used and evidence of their accuracy;
- The number, duration and results of samples taken;
- The type of personal protective equipment used (e.g., type of respirators worn); and
- The name, social security number and job classification of all workers represented by the monitoring, specifying which workers were actually monitored.

Historical Monitoring Data

When an employer relies on historical monitoring data to determine worker exposures to Cr(VI), an accurate record of the historical monitoring data must be maintained. The record must show:

- That the data was collected using methods that meet the accuracy requirements of the standard;
- That the processes and work practices, characteristics of the Cr(VI)-containing material, and environmental conditions at the time the data was obtained are essentially the same as those of the job for which current exposure is being determined; and
- Any other relevant data regarding operations, materials, processes, or worker exposures.

Objective Data

When an employer relies on objective data to comply with the Cr(VI) standard, an accurate record of the objective data must be maintained. The record must indicate:

- The Cr(VI)-containing material in question;
- The source of the objective data;
- The testing protocol and results of testing, or analysis of the material for the release of Cr(VI);
- A description of the process, operation, or activity and how the data support the determination; and
- Any other relevant data regarding the processes, operations, activities, materials, or worker exposures.

Medical Surveillance

The employer must maintain an accurate record for each worker provided medical surveillance under the standard. The record must include the following information about the worker:

- Name and social security number;
- A copy of the PLHCP's written opinions; and
- A copy of the information that the employer was required to provide to the PLHCP (i.e., a description of the worker's duties as they relate to occupational Cr(VI) exposure; the worker's Cr(VI) exposure levels; a description of the personal protective equipment used by the worker; and information from previous employment-related medical examinations).

Exposure and medical records must be maintained and made available to workers and their representatives in accordance with 29 CFR 1910.1020, Access to Employee Exposure and Medical Records. In general, exposure records must be kept for at least 30 years, and medical records must be kept for the duration of employment plus 30 years. It is necessary to keep these records for extended periods because cancer often cannot be detected until 20 or more years after exposure, and exposure and medical records can assist in diagnosing and identifying the cause of disease.

Effective Dates

All provisions of the standard are currently in effect, except that employers have until May 31, 2010 to implement required engineering controls.

Additional Information

Small Entity Compliance Guide for the Hexavalent Chromium Standards:
www.osha.gov/Publications/OSHA_small_entity_comp.pdf

Small Entity Compliance Guide for the Revised Respiratory Protection Standard:
www.osha.gov/Publications/3384small-entity-for-respiratory-protection-standard-rev.pdf

OSHA Fact Sheet: Health Effects of Hexavalent Chromium:
www.osha.gov/OshDoc/data_General_Facts/hexavalent_chromium.pdf

Hexavalent Chromium General Industry standard:
www.osha.gov/pls/oshaweb/owadisp.show_document?p_table=STANDARDS&p_id=13096

Hexavalent Chromium Shipyard standard:
www.osha.gov/pls/oshaweb/owadisp.show_document?p_table=STANDARDS&p_id=13116

Hexavalent Chromium Construction standard:
www.osha.gov/pls/oshaweb/owadisp.show_document?p_table=ST
ANDARDS&p_id=13117

For a list of State plans and contact information:
www.osha.gov/dcsp/osp/index.html.

References

Meridian Research, Inc. 1994. Final Report: Selected Chapters of
an Economic Impact Analysis for a Revised OSHA Standard for
Chromium VI: Introduction, Industry Profiles, Exposure Profiles,
Technological Feasibility (for 6 industries) and Environmental
Impacts. Prepared for: Office of Regulatory Analysis, OSHA,
Prepared by: Meridian Research, Inc., Prepared under Contract
Number: J-9-F-4-0012, Task Order No. 1, Base Year, December 18,
1994, pages I-2 through I-7, Document ID Number OSHA-H054A-
2006-0064-0720 (formerly Exhibit Number 26).

OSHA. 2003. Clarification of "as free as practicable" and lead contamination under 29 CFR 1926.62. OSHA's Letter of Interpretation
response to Mr. Frank White of Organization Resources
Counselors, Inc. January 13, 2003.

OSHA. 2006. Occupational Exposure to Hexavalent Chromium.
Final Rule. 71 FR 10099-10385. 2/28/2006.

OSHA Instruction. 2008. Inspection Procedures for the Chromium
(VI) Standards. Directive Number: CPL 02-02-074. Effective Date:
January 24, 2008.

SRI Consulting. 2008. Chemical Economics Handbook. Inorganic
Color Pigments. CEH Marketing Research Report. January 2008,
pages 575.3002A through 575.3002J.

OSHA Assistance

OSHA can provide extensive help through a variety of programs, including technical assistance about effective safety and health programs, state plans, workplace consultations, and training and education.

Safety and Health Management System Guidelines

Effective management of worker safety and health protection is a decisive factor in reducing the extent and severity of work-related injuries and illnesses and their related costs. In fact, an effective safety and health management system forms the basis of good worker protection, can save time and money, increase productivity and reduce employee injuries, illnesses and related workers' compensation costs.

To assist employers and workers in developing effective safety and health management systems, OSHA published recommended Safety and Health Program Management Guidelines (54 *Federal Register* (16): 3904-3916, January 26, 1989). These voluntary guidelines can be applied to all places of employment covered by OSHA.

The guidelines identify four general elements critical to the development of a successful safety and health management system:

- Management leadership and worker involvement,
- Worksite analysis,
- Hazard prevention and control, and
- Safety and health training.

The guidelines recommend specific actions, under each of these general elements, to achieve an effective safety and health management system. The *Federal Register* notice is available online at www.osha.gov.

State Programs

The Occupational Safety and Health Act of 1970 (OSH Act) encourages states to develop and operate their own job safety and health plans. Twenty-four states, Puerto Rico and the Virgin

Islands currently operate approved state plans: 22 cover both private and public (state and local government) employment; Connecticut, New Jersey, New York and the Virgin Islands cover the public sector only. States and territories with their own OSHA-approved occupational safety and health plans must adopt standards identical to, or at least as effective as, the Federal OSHA standards.

Consultation Services

Consultation assistance is available on request to employers who want help in establishing and maintaining a safe and healthful workplace. Largely funded by OSHA, the service is provided at no cost to the employer. Primarily developed for smaller employers with more hazardous operations, the consultation service is delivered by state governments employing professional safety and health consultants. Comprehensive assistance includes an appraisal of all mechanical systems, work practices and occupational safety and health hazards of the workplace and all aspects of the employer's present job safety and health program. In addition, the service offers assistance to employers in developing and implementing an effective safety and health program. No penalties are proposed or citations issued for hazards identified by the consultant. OSHA provides consultation assistance to the employer with the assurance that his or her name and firm and any information about the workplace will not be routinely reported to OSHA enforcement staff. For more information concerning consultation assistance, see OSHA's website at www.osha.gov.

Strategic Partnership Program

OSHA's Strategic Partnership Program helps encourage, assist and recognize the efforts of partners to eliminate serious workplace hazards and achieve a high level of worker safety and health. Most strategic partnerships seek to have a broad impact by building cooperative relationships with groups of employers and workers. These partnerships are voluntary relationships between OSHA, employers, worker representatives, and others (e.g., trade unions, trade and professional associations, universities, and other government agencies).

For more information on this and other agency programs, contact your nearest OSHA office, or visit OSHA's website at www.osha.gov.

OSHA Training and Education

OSHA area offices offer a variety of information services, such as technical advice, publications, audiovisual aids and speakers for special engagements. OSHA's Training Institute in Arlington Heights, IL, provides basic and advanced courses in safety and health for Federal and state compliance officers, state consultants, Federal agency personnel, and private sector employers, workers and their representatives.

The OSHA Training Institute also has established OSHA Training Institute Education Centers to address the increased demand for its courses from the private sector and from other federal agencies. These centers are colleges, universities and nonprofit organizations that have been selected after a competition for participation in the program.

OSHA also provides funds to nonprofit organizations, through grants, to conduct workplace training and education in subjects where OSHA believes there is a lack of workplace training. Grants are awarded annually.

For more information on grants, training and education, contact the OSHA Training Institute, Directorate of Training and Education, 2020 South Arlington Heights Road, Arlington Heights, IL 60005, (847) 297-4810, or see Training on OSHA's website at www.osha.gov. For further information on any OSHA program, contact your nearest OSHA regional office listed at the end of this publication.

Information Available Electronically

OSHA has a variety of materials and tools available on its website at www.osha.gov. These include electronic tools, such as *Safety and Health Topics*, *eTools*, *Expert Advisors*; regulations, directives and publications; videos and other information for employers and workers. OSHA's software programs and eTools walk you through challenging safety and health issues and common problems to find the best solutions for your workplace.

OSHA Publications

OSHA has an extensive publications program. For a listing of free items, visit OSHA's website at www.osha.gov or contact the OSHA Publications Office, U.S. Department of Labor, 200 Constitution Avenue, NW, N-3101, Washington, DC 20210; telephone (202) 693-1888 or fax to (202) 693-2498.

Contacting OSHA

To report an emergency, file a complaint, or seek OSHA advice, assistance, or products, call (800) 321-OSHA or contact your nearest OSHA Regional or Area office listed at the end of this publication. The teletypewriter (TTY) number is (877) 889-5627.

Written correspondence can be mailed to the nearest OSHA Regional or Area Office listed at the end of this publication or to OSHA's national office at: U.S. Department of Labor, Occupational Safety and Health Administration, 200 Constitution Avenue, N.W., Washington, DC 20210.

By visiting OSHA's website at www.osha.gov, you can also:

▪ File a complaint online,

▪ Submit general inquiries about workplace safety and health electronically, and

▪ Find more information about OSHA and occupational safety and health.

OSHA Regional Offices

Region I
(CT*, ME, MA, NH, RI, VT*)
JFK Federal Building, Room E340
Boston, MA 02203
(617) 565-9860

Region II
(NJ*, NY*, PR*, VI*)
201 Varick Street, Room 670
New York, NY 10014
(212) 337-2378

Region III
(DE, DC, MD*, PA, VA*, WV)
The Curtis Center
170 S. Independence Mall West
Suite 740 West
Philadelphia, PA 19106-3309
(215) 861-4900

Region IV
(AL, FL, GA, KY*, MS, NC*, SC*, TN*)
61 Forsyth Street, SW, Room 6T50
Atlanta, GA 30303
(404) 562-2300

Region V
(IL*, IN*, MI*, MN*, OH, WI)
230 South Dearborn Street
Room 3244
Chicago, IL 60604
(312) 353-2220

Region VI
(AR, LA, NM*, OK, TX)
525 Griffin Street, Room 602
Dallas, TX 75202
(972) 850-4145

Region VII
(IA*, KS, MO, NE)
Two Pershing Square
2300 Main Street, Suite 1010
Kansas City, MO 64108-2416
(816) 283-8745

Region VIII
(CO, MT, NO, SO, UT*, WY*)
1999 Broadway, Suite 1690
PO Box 46550
Denver, CO 80202-5716
(720) 264-6550

Region IX
(AZ*, CA*, HI*, NV,* and American
Samoa, Guam and the Northern
Mariana Islands)
90 7th Street, Suite 18-100
San Francisco, CA 94103
(415) 625-2547

Region X
(AK*, ID, OR*, WA*)
1111 Third Avenue, Suite 715
Seattle, WA 98101-3212
(206) 553-5930

* These states and territories operate their own OSHA-approved job safety and health programs and cover state and local government employees as well as private sector employees. The Connecticut, Illinois, New Jersey, New York and Virgin Islands plans cover public employees only. States with approved programs must have standards that are identical to, or at least as effective as, the Federal OSHA standards.

Note: To get contact information for OSHA Area Offices, OSHA-approved State Plans and OSHA Consultation Projects, please visit us online at www.osha.gov or call us at 1-800-321-0SHA.